Instant PostgreSQL Backup and Restore How-to

A step-by-step guide to backing up and restoring your database using safe, efficient, and proven recipes

Shaun M. Thomas

BIRMINGHAM - MUMBAI

Instant PostgreSQL Backup and Restore How-to

First published: March 2013

Production Reference: 1200313

Published by Packt Publishing Ltd.
Livery Place
35 Livery Street
Birmingham B3 2PB, UK.

ISBN 978-1-78216-910-9

www.packtpub.com

Credits

Author
Shaun M. Thomas

Reviewers
Peter Eisentraut
Robert H. Treat

Acquisition Editor
Martin Bell

Commissioning Editor
Yogesh Dalvi

Technical Editor
Veena Pagare

Copy Editor
Laxmi Subramanian

Project Coordinator
Sneha Modi

Proofreader
Maria Gould

Production Coordinator
Melwyn D'sa

Cover Work
Melwyn D'sa

Cover Image
Sheetal Aute

About the Author

Shaun M. Thomas has been a database administrator for a long time, and has been working with PostgreSQL since late 2000. Over the years, he has contributed frequently to the PostgreSQL performance mailing list to help other DBAs get the most out of his favorite database. In 2011 and 2012, he presented at the Postgres Open conference on topics such as handling extreme throughput, high availability, server redundancy, and failover techniques.

Currently, he serves as the database architect at OptionsHouse, an online options brokerage with a PostgreSQL database that handles over one billion queries per day. This database, he says, is proof that PostgreSQL is ready for the big time.

He has great hopes for PostgreSQL as it continues to break new ground and make history.

About the Reviewers

Peter Eisentraut is a member of the core team of the PostgreSQL project and has over a decade of experience in developing and operating PostgreSQL applications. He is also active in Debian and other open source projects.

Robert Treat has been building database-backed, Internet-oriented systems for over a decade. A long time developer, user, and advocate for open source technologies, he has contributed to dozens of open source projects over the years, and has been recognized as a major contributor to the PostgreSQL project. An international speaker on open source, databases, and web operations, he spends his days as COO at OmniTI, a consultancy focused on developing and managing web systems at scale.

www.PacktPub.com

Support files, eBooks, discount offers and more

You might want to visit `www.PacktPub.com` for support files and downloads related to your book.

Did you know that Packt offers eBook versions of every book published, with PDF and ePub files available? You can upgrade to the eBook version at `www.PacktPub.com` and as a print book customer, you are entitled to a discount on the eBook copy. Get in touch with us at `service@packtpub.com` for more details.

At `www.PacktPub.com`, you can also read a collection of free technical articles, sign up for a range of free newsletters and receive exclusive discounts and offers on Packt books and eBooks.

`http://PacktLib.PacktPub.com`

Do you need instant solutions to your IT questions? PacktLib is Packt's online digital book library. Here, you can access, read and search across Packt's entire library of books.

Why Subscribe?

- ▸ Fully searchable across every book published by Packt
- ▸ Copy and paste, print and bookmark content
- ▸ On demand and accessible via web browser

Free Access for Packt account holders

If you have an account with Packt at `www.PacktPub.com`, you can use this to access PacktLib today and view nine entirely free books. Simply use your login credentials for immediate access.

Table of Contents

Preface

Welcome to *Instant PostgreSQL Backup and Restore How-to*! These days, database-driven websites and applications are everywhere. Thanks to its free and open nature, and in no small part due to its full ACID guarantees, PostgreSQL is now a popular RDBMS used to fill the role of data storage in these next-generation apps. But with great power comes great responsibility. For a conscientious DBA, that means robust and sometimes numerous backups.

That's where we come in. PostgreSQL supplies a good toolset and documentation for securing your data from catastrophic loss. But this documentation is meant to be exhaustive, covering every known variant of using the backup tools. In a hurry? A new PostgreSQL DBA? Wading through all of that information might be overwhelming. It's there for long-term reference, not immediate or simple solutions.

This How-to fills the missing role of simple explanations for managing backups. We have a small recipe for each major variant of backup, and how to restore it. That's all. Just some commands you might type, and some exposition on how it works. No matter the size of your installation, something in this book should address your needs.

What this book covers

Getting a basic export gives an easy solution for small databases. All good things have a beginning. Export your entire database installation with a single command. Compress it and save it for later.

Partial database exports covers the tools that offer finer-grained control over what data you receive, making data migrations and copies possible. Larger databases are often backed up piece by piece.

Restoring a database export, combined with the previous recipe, has a complete solution for backup management. What to do with the backups you've made so far, and how to import them quickly is taken care of by backup management.

Obtaining a binary backup will cover the easiest way to get an exact copy of the database files for things such as warm or hot standby, or streaming replication, and open up several new possibilities. More complex systems need that copy of the database.

Stepping into TAR backups will cover parallel compression, so your backups become faster than what the default tools can provide. `tar` files are a Unix staple. They can also produce binary backups with the help of a couple of database commands.

Taking Snapshots will cover basic filesystem snapshots to freeze data files in place, and prevent partial or corrupt backups. Sometimes the filesystem itself can aid your backup efforts.

Synchronize backup servers will cover the basic tools to copy the data to a new server, and how to keep the data in sync afterwards. Larger installations should have multiple online copies of the database. The first step is to copy the data to a new server.

Restoring a binary backup will cover the methods of restoring the data files. With all those methods of backing up data files, we also need to restore them properly. It's not as easy as extracting the files and starting the database, but it's close.

Point in time recovery will tell you how to restore your data to a specific point in its history as if any problem never occurred. More complex restore situations may require stopping the restore before some catastrophic problem or data mismanagement.

Warm and hot standby will tell you how to make a backup of a complete online server. In an enterprise, having a complete online server can save millions in worst-case scenarios. It's the backup that can take over in case of emergencies.

Streaming replication covers how to use your backup(s) as secondary servers. The ultimate online backup is one that is never truly out of sync. Every transaction is copied when completed, and in some cases, guaranteed to exist on the remote server.

What you need for this book

This How-to is focused on Unix systems with a primary Linux focus. The LAMP (Linux, Apache, MySQL, PHP) stack of services is often modified to LAPP (Linux, Apache, PostgreSQL, PHP). This type of server makes up a large majority of hobbyist usage and several Enterprise-level systems. We highly recommend you to have a virtual machine or development system running a recent copy of Debian, Ubuntu, Red Hat Enterprise Linux, or a variant such as CentOS or Scientific Linux.

You will also need a copy of PostgreSQL. Though most Linux distributions include PostgreSQL packages, they are often one or more versions behind. So we recommend going to the PostgreSQL website, and downloading a copy that matches the architecture you have chosen. You can find these at the following URL:

```
http://www.postgresql.org/download/
```

Be sure to include the contrib packages in your installation. They include helpful utilities such as a benchmark suite, which we will be using in our recipes to generate sample data.

If you have a BSD system, you should still be able to follow along. Some commands may need to be altered to run properly on BSD, so be sure to understand the intent before executing them. All commands have been confirmed to work on BASH and recent GNU tools.

Who this book is for

This book is for anyone (and everyone) running PostgreSQL on a server. Your data is important, as losing it without proper backups can mean long nights, lost business, and in extreme cases, shutting down the company.

PostgreSQL DBAs are encouraged to use this resource for the advanced recipes.

Companies without a DBA may have a greater need, since the remaining system administrators and developers probably lack PostgreSQL expertise. If you are such a developer or system administrator, we highly recommend you to use the techniques we describe to prevent unnecessary risk. Who knows, you may even have a future as a PostgreSQL DBA!

Conventions

In this book, you will find a number of styles of text that distinguish between different kinds of information. Here are some examples of these styles, and an explanation of their meaning.

Code words in text are shown as follows: "We can use the `createdb` utility to create an empty database for our backup experimentation."

A block of code is set as follows:

```
for f in $(find /db/pg_tblspc); do
    d=$(readlink -f $f)
    n=$(basename $f)
    tar -C $d . -c | pigz -p 8 > /backup/$n.tar.gz
done
```

Any command-line input or output is written as follows:

```
$> export PGUSER=postgres
$> createdb sample
$> pgbench -i -s 50 sample
```

New terms and **important words** are shown in bold. Words that you see on the screen, in menus or dialog boxes for example, appear in the text like this: "Clicking the **Next** button moves you to the next screen".

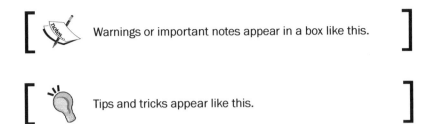

Warnings or important notes appear in a box like this.

Tips and tricks appear like this.

Reader feedback

Feedback from our readers is always welcome. Let us know what you think about this book—what you liked or may have disliked. Reader feedback is important for us to develop titles that you really get the most out of.

To send us general feedback, simply send an e-mail to feedback@packtpub.com, and mention the book title via the subject of your message.

If there is a topic that you have expertise in and you are interested in either writing or contributing to a book, see our author guide on www.packtpub.com/authors.

Customer support

Now that you are the proud owner of a Packt book, we have a number of things to help you to get the most from your purchase.

Errata

Although we have taken every care to ensure the accuracy of our content, mistakes do happen. If you find a mistake in one of our books—maybe a mistake in the text or the code—we would be grateful if you would report this to us. By doing so, you can save other readers from frustration and help us improve subsequent versions of this book. If you find any errata, please report them by visiting http://www.packtpub.com/submit-errata, selecting your book, clicking on the **errata submission form** link, and entering the details of your errata. Once your errata are verified, your submission will be accepted and the errata will be uploaded on our website, or added to any list of existing errata, under the Errata section of that title. Any existing errata can be viewed by selecting your title from http://www.packtpub.com/support.

Piracy

Piracy of copyright material on the Internet is an ongoing problem across all media. At Packt, we take the protection of our copyright and licenses very seriously. If you come across any illegal copies of our works, in any form, on the Internet, please provide us with the location address or website name immediately so that we can pursue a remedy.

Please contact us at `copyright@packtpub.com` with a link to the suspected pirated material.

We appreciate your help in protecting our authors, and our ability to bring you valuable content.

Questions

You can contact us at `questions@packtpub.com` if you are having a problem with any aspect of the book, and we will do our best to address it.

Instant PostgreSQL Backup and Restore How-to

Welcome to *PostgreSQL Backup and Restore How-to*. Here, we'll explore the proper, secure, and reliable methods for preserving mission-critical data. More importantly, we'll tell you how to get that data back! PostgreSQL provides several handy tools for both basic SQL exports and binary backup, which we will combine with more advanced techniques for a complete toolkit. By the end of this book, you should have a full array of options that you can automate for worry-free backups.

Getting a basic export (Simple)

We will start with `pg_dumpall`, the most basic PostgreSQL backup tool. This single command-line utility can export the entire database instance at once. We want to start with this particular command, because it preserves important information such as users, roles, and passwords. Later, we will only use it to obtain this important metadata.

Getting ready

Before we begin backing up our database, we should have a database! Since we have installed both PostgreSQL and the Contrib tools, we should have everything we need to get started with. To make things easier, we will export a single environment variable to run all commands as the postgres user. This user owns the database instance in default installs. Exporting this variable lets you act as the postgres user for all future examples. Later, we can use the createdb utility to create an empty database for our backup experimentation. The pgbench utility will be our source of data, as shown in the following code snippet, since backing up an empty database is hard to verify upon restore:

```
$> export PGUSER=postgres
$> createdb sample
$> pgbench -i -s 50 sample
```

Now we have a database named sample with several tables full of generated data. Since the default row count for the tool is 100,000, a scale of 50 provides a table with five million rows that we can use to verify the backup processing time required. We can also verify the restored database by checking for the existence of the generated tables and their content. If this scale is too large, feel free to use a smaller scale to follow along.

> The sample database will be the basis for all subsequent data export examples. Unless otherwise specified, it always starts with a fresh database. Again, you can use the suggested scale size here, or choose your own.

How to do it...

Creating a backup this way requires a single command, as follows:

1. Make sure you have opened a **Command Prompt** console as a local user on your Linux system, and type the following command:

```
$> pg_dumpall -f backup.sql
```

How it works...

The pg_dumpall utility produces what should be a full copy of all database objects including users, schemas, and data, as a single very large SQL file. Our example directed the SQL output to a file named backup.sql, but any name is valid, so long as we can remember it later.

There's more...

Though the venerable `--help` command-line switch always lists the full capabilities available to us, the more important of these deserve more discussion.

Restoring the export

Before we get much further, we should quickly explain how to restore the SQL file you just produced. Our other recipes are more complex and require separate sections, but restoring a `pg_dumpall` export is very easy. The `psql` command is used for running SQL files. Since this is just a SQL file, you can run it directly against the database. Try the following:

```
$> psql -f backup.sql postgres
```

The `-f` switch tells PostgreSQL that we want to execute our backup file against the database `postgres`, which is a placeholder. The `psql` command expects a database name, so we have provided a simple default. Your backup will still restore properly, for example, creating and filling the sample database. This is because the backup also contains database creation commands and more commands to change database targets so that all data goes where it should. Like we said, this is the easiest backup method PostgreSQL has.

Exporting global objects

Though the SQL export itself is perfectly valid for restore, many administrators prefer to use the `pg_dumpall` export to obtain the globally stored objects such as `users`, `roles`, and `passwords` only, and use other tools for things such as tables and other data. To get this global data alone, the `-g` switch tells `pg_dumpall` that is all we wanted. Type the following command to get only global objects:

```
$> pg_dumpall -g -f globals.sql
```

We will be using the previous command frequently for just getting global objects.

Compressed backups

Unfortunately `pg_dumpall` cannot directly compress its output; it is a very basic tool. If we have an extremely large database, other UNIX commands will also be necessary. For example, the following command will compress the dump using a parallel algorithm while it is being produced, to greatly reduce backup time and size:

```
$> pg_dumpall | gzip > backup.sql.gz
```

Naming backups

Note that in all of our examples thus far, we have named the backup rather poorly. It is a better practice to use the `-f` switch to provide a name that follows a specific naming scheme. Backup files should always include at least one contextual clue, the date on which the backup was taken, and possibly the time. The following is a better example:

```
$> pg_dumpall -f production_2013-02-15.sql
```

Partial database exports (Simple)

Backups are not limited to the whole running instance. Each database can be dumped individually with the `pg_dump` utility.

Getting ready

Please refer to the *Getting a basic export (Simple)* recipe on preparing a `sample` database.

How to do it...

This time, we will need to execute the following commands on the command line:

1. First, type the following command to obtain global objects such as `users`, `groups`, and `passwords`:

   ```
   $> pg_dumpall -g -f globals.sql
   ```

2. Next, this command will create a `sample` database:

   ```
   $> pg_dump -f sample_backup.sql sample
   ```

How it works...

This took a bit more effort, but not much. Because the `pg_dump` utility can only back up one database at a time, we don't get global objects such as `users` and `groups`. Thus we must also use `pg_dumpall` if we want to restore with the same users and groups.

But what about the SQL dump itself? Just like `pg_dumpall`, `pg_dump` uses the `-f` switch to send output to a named file. The last parameter is a positional parameter. Most PostgreSQL tools are set up to assume the last parameter without a flag is actually a database name. In this case, our `sample` database is what we are exporting to SQL.

There's more...

Why do we even need `pg_dump` if it can only back up one database at a time? It seems silly at first, but by doing so, we unlock several additional capabilities, not the least of which is the ability to *restore* a database independently of its original name. There are also significant improvements and several new command-line options.

Compressed exports

Unlike `pg_dumpall`, which could not compress backup output, `pg_dump` makes it quite simple by using the following command:

```
$> pg_dump -Fc -f sample_backup.pgr sample
```

The `-F` switch changes the output format. In this case, we chose `c` for custom output. The PostgreSQL custom output format is a proprietary compressed export that you will not be able to read, but requires much less space than the default SQL output. The restore tool actually prefers this format, and requires it for advanced options such as parallel database restore, which we will be discussing later.

Table-only exports

Not only can we restrict a backup to a single database, but `pg_dump` also provides an option to back up one or more tables. Our `sample` database contains a `pgbench_accounts` table. Let's export this table by itself with the following command:

```
$> pg_dump -t pgbench_accounts -f accounts_backup.sql sample
```

Exporting individual tables means they can also be restored in other databases or archived for later. We can also use the `-t` switch as often as we like, keeping several related tables together. However, keep in mind that getting a complete list of related tables is often difficult. Views, triggers, stored procedures, and other related objects may also be necessary to retain full functionality of these objects upon restore. When you use this option, you only get the objects you requested, and nothing else.

Schema-only exports

As with tables, schemas themselves (collections of related objects) can be exported. Our `sample` database only has the `public` schema, which we can export with the `-n` switch, as shown in the following command:

```
$> pg_dump -n public -f public_namespace_backup.sql sample
```

Larger instances sometimes have schemas for each application or client. With the option to export these separately, they can be moved between databases, backed up or restored independently of the entire database, or archived.

Data and schema-only exports

Tables, views, and other objects contained in the schema can also be exported with or without the data. Perhaps we want to track schema changes, for example, as shown in the following command:

```
$> pg_dump -s -f schema_backup.sql sample
```

The opposite is also true. We may not need or want the schema definitions. The -a flag gives us only table data using the following command:

```
$> pg_dump -a -f data_backup.sql sample
```

Again, remember that performing an export of a single object may lose a lot of dependent elements (for example, views). Don't use the single object export options if you need this information together.

Either of these options can be combined with table or schema exports. Let's grab only the data for the pgbench_branches table.

```
$> pg_dump -a -t pgbench_branches -f branch_data.sql sample
```

Restoring a database export (Simple)

Once a backup is taken, we need to know how to use it to restore the database to working order. Once again, PostgreSQL provides the pg_restore utility to do all of the hard work.

Getting ready

Please refer to the *Getting a basic export (Simple)* recipe on preparing a sample database. The pg_restore tool gains the most functionality with the **custom** export format, so we will use that for the following example. These commands should produce a simple SQL export of our databases. We will give the backup a .pgr extension, indicating that it is a PostgreSQL backup file, as shown in the following command:

```
$> pg_dump -Fc -f sample_backup.pgr sample
$> pg_dumpall -g -f globals.sql
```

Once these files are safely stored elsewhere, revert the database to a fresh install.

The normal procedure to do this is a bit complex, so for now, we can cheat a little. Simply drop the sample database with the following command, and we can continue:

```
$> dropdb sample
```

How to do it...

The `pg_restore` tool is not quite analogous to `pg_dump`. It is more of a sophisticated backup playback engine. Since we are working with a partial export, there are a few extra steps to fully restore everything as follows:

1. Again, start by obtaining our global objects:

   ```
   $> psql -f globals.sql postgres
   ```

2. Next, create the sample database:

   ```
   $> createdb sample
   ```

3. Finally, use the following restoration command:

   ```
   $> pg_restore -d sample sample_backup.pgr
   ```

How it works...

There is a bit of new material here. We started by using the `psql` utility to execute commands in the `globals.sql` file. Remember, output of `pg_dumpall` is just in SQL format, so we can use PostgreSQL's default SQL execution command. We can connect to the `postgres` database, since it always exists as a root for new database installations. This creates the global objects such as `users` and `groups` that we always want to preserve.

We then needed the `sample` database to exist, so we used `createdb`, another PostgreSQL utility we have used before. This time, it provides a target for `pg_restore`. By using the `-d` flag, our backup is restored directly into the `sample` database instead of any preexisting defaults. The last parameter is similar to how we specify a database name with `pg_dump` or `psql`. But for `pg_restore`, the last unnamed parameter is assumed to be a database backup to restore.

There's more...

That was admittedly much more complicated than simply using `pg_dumpall` to export everything, and `psql` to restore it including database names. However, now we are using much more powerful tools and gaining even further flexibility.

Parallel database restore

Since we are using PostgreSQL Version 8.4 or higher, the `pg_restore` utility includes the ability to execute parts of a backup file in parallel. While data is restoring in one table, indexes could be created in another. We could have restored our `sample` database using the following command:

```
$> pg_restore -j 4 -d sample sample_backup.pgr
```

This would invoke four restore jobs (-j) simultaneously. With enough CPUs, restores finish several times faster than the default linear process. Index and primary key creation are very CPU intensive.

Database targeting

Note how we always specify the restore database. We could just as easily restore the database twice with different names each time! Each database is independent of the other. The following command lines show how we can restore the database twice:

```
$> createdb sample
$> createdb extra
$> pg_restore -d sample sample_backup.pgr
$> pg_restore -d extra sample_backup.pgr
```

This is a perfect tool to experiment with production data safely or to restore an old backup next to a production database, and transfer data between them.

Partial database restores

Even though our export is of the entire sample database, we could restore only portions of it, or only the schema, or only the data. Much like pg_dump, all these options are available, and pg_restore is smart enough to ignore irrelevant parts of a source backup. The following command would only restore the pgbench_tellers table:

```
$> pg_restore -d sample -t pgbench_tellers sample_backup.pgr
```

 Remember to create your databases with createdb before restoring them!

Obtaining a binary backup (Simple)

Another backup method available to PostgreSQL is a base backup, which consists of the actual data files themselves. These kinds of backups do not need to be restored, only uncompressed or copied. Using them can be more complicated, but they can be ready much faster depending on the database size. The developers have kindly provided pg_basebackup as a simple starting point.

Getting ready

Please refer to the *Getting a basic export (Simple)* recipe on preparing a sample database.

Next we need to modify the `postgresql.conf` file for our database to run in the proper mode for this type of backup. Change the following configuration variables:

```
wal_level = archive
max_wal_senders = 5
```

Then we must allow a super user to connect to the `replication` database, which is used by `pg_basebackup`. We do that by adding the following line to `pg_hba.conf`:

```
local replication postgres peer
```

Finally, restart the `database` instance to commit the changes.

How to do it...

Though it is only one command, `pg_basebackup` requires at least one switch to obtain a binary backup, as shown in the following step:

1. Execute the following command to create the backup in a new directory named db_backup:

    ```
    $> pg_basebackup -D db_backup -x
    ```

How it works...

For PostgreSQL, **WAL** stands for **Write Ahead Log**. By changing `wal_level` to `archive`, those logs are written in a format compatible with `pg_basebackup` and other replication-based tools.

By increasing `max_wal_senders` from the default of zero, the database will allow tools to connect and request data files. In this case, up to five streams can request data files simultaneously. This maximum should be sufficient for all but the most advanced systems.

The `pg_hba.conf` file is essentially a connection **access control list** (**ACL**). Since `pg_basebackup` uses the replication protocol to obtain data files, we need to allow local connections to request replication.

Next, we send the backup itself to a directory (`-D`) named db_backup. This directory will effectively contain a complete copy of the binary files that make up the database.

Finally, we added the `-x` flag to include transaction logs (`xlogs`), which the database will require to start, if we want to use this backup. When we get into more complex scenarios, we will exclude this option, but for now, it greatly simplifies the process.

There's more...

The `pg_basebackup` tool is actually fairly complicated. There is a lot more involved under the hood.

Viewing backup progress

For manually invoked backups, we may want to know how long the process might take, and its current status. Luckily, `pg_basebackup` has a progress indicator, which does that by using the following command:

```
$> pg_basebackup -P -D db_backup
```

Like many of the other switches, `-P` can be combined with tape archive format, standalone backups, database clones, and so on. This is clearly not necessary for automated backup routines, but could be useful for one-off backups monitored by an administrator.

Compressed tape archive backups

Many binary backup files come in the **TAR** (**Tape Archive**) format, which we can activate using the `-f` flag and setting it to `t` for TAR. Several Unix backup tools can directly process this type of backup, and most administrators are familiar with it.

If we want a compressed output, we can set the `-z` flag, especially in the case of large databases. For our `sample` database, we should see almost a 20x compression ratio. Try the following command:

```
$> pg_basebackup -Ft -z -D db_backup
```

The backup file itself will be named `base.tar.gz` within the `db_backup` directory, reflecting its status as a compressed tape archive. In case the database contains extra tablespaces, each becomes a separate compressed archive. Each file can be extracted to a separate location, such as a different set of disks, for very complicated database instances.

For the sake of this example, we ignored the possible presence of extra tablespaces than the `pg_default` default included in every installation. User-created tablespaces will greatly complicate your backup process.

Making the backup standalone

By specifying `-x`, we tell the database that we want a "complete" backup. This means we could extract or copy the backup anywhere and start it as a fully qualified database. As we mentioned before, the flag means that you want to include transaction logs, which is how the database recovers from crashes, checks integrity, and performs other important tasks. The following is the command again, for reference:

```
$> pg_basebackup -x -D db_backup
```

When combined with the TAR output format and compression, standalone binary backups are perfect for archiving to tape for later retrieval, as each backup is compressed and self-contained. By default, `pg_basebackup` does not include transaction logs, because many (possibly most) administrators back these up separately. These files have multiple uses, and putting them in the basic backup would duplicate efforts and make backups larger than necessary.

We include them at this point because it is still too early for such complicated scenarios. We will get there eventually, of course.

Database clones

Because `pg_basebackup` operates through PostgreSQL's replication protocol, it can execute remotely. For instance, if the database was on a server named `Production`, and we wanted a copy on a server named `Recovery`, we could execute the following command from `Recovery`:

```
$> pg_basebackup -h Production -x -D /full/db/path
```

For this to work, we would also need this line in `pg_hba.conf` for `Recovery`:

```
    host replication postgres Recovery trust
```

Though we set the authentication method to `trust`, this is not recommended for a production server installation. However, it is sufficient to allow `Recovery` to copy all data from `Production`. With the `-x` flag, it also means that the database can be started and kept online in case of emergency. It is a backup *and* a running server.

Parallel compression

Compression is very CPU intensive, but there are some utilities capable of threading the process. Tools such as `pbzip2` or `pigz` can do the compression instead. Unfortunately, this only works in the case of a single tablespace (the default one; if you create more, this will not work). The following is the command for compression using `pigz`:

```
$> pg_basebackup -Ft -D - | pigz -j 4 > db_backup.tar.gz
```

It uses four threads of compression, and sets the backup directory to standard output (`-`) so that `pigz` can process the output itself.

Stepping into TAR backups (Intermediate)

For a very long time, the Unix `tar` command was one of the only methods for obtaining a full binary backup of a PostgreSQL database. This is still the case for more advanced installations which may make use of filesystem snapshots, extensively utilize tablespaces, or otherwise disrupt the included management tools. For these advanced scenarios and more, `tar` is indispensable for circumventing or augmenting the provided tools.

Getting ready

Please refer to the *Getting a basic export (Simple)* recipe on preparing a `sample` database.

For the purposes of this example, we will assume that the database directory is /db, and the archived files will go to /archive. Based on this, we need to modify the postgresql.conf file to archive transaction logs during the backup. Change the following configuration variables:

```
archive_mode = on
archive_command = 'test -f /archive/%f || cp %p /archive/%f'
```

After PostgreSQL is restarted, the database will be ready for a tar backup.

How to do it...

Creating a tar backup is done with the following three basic steps, plus a fourth set of commands that are considered as good practice:

1. First, tell PostgreSQL to enter backup mode:

   ```
   $> psql -c "SELECT pg_start_backup('label');" postgres
   ```

2. Next, we produce the actual backup with tar, instead of pg_dump or pg_basebackup:

   ```
   $> tar -c -z -f backup.tar.gz /db
   ```

3. Finally, we tell the database to end backup mode:

   ```
   $> psql -c "SELECT pg_stop_backup();" postgres
   ```

4. We also need the transaction logs archived during the backup. Type these commands as shown:

   ```
   $> recent=$(ls -r /archive/*.backup | head -1)
   $> bstart=$(grep 'START WAL' $recent | sed 's/.* //; s/)//;')
   $> echo $bstart > /tmp/MANIFEST
   $> echo $recent >> /tmp/MANIFEST
   $> find /archive -newer /archive/$bstart \
      ! -newer $recent >> /tmp/FILES
   $> sed 's%/.*/%%' /tmp/MANIFEST | sort | uniq \
      > /archive/MANIFEST
   $> tar -C /archive -cz -f archive.tar.gz \
      --files-from=/archive/MANIFEST
   ```

Obviously, much of this can (and should) be scripted. These commands were designed for a standard Linux system. If you are using BSD or another variant, you many need to convert them before doing this yourself.

How it works...

The `tar` command for creating a backup itself is fairly simple: creating (`-c`) a `.gzip` compressed (`-z`) file named `backup.tar.gz` from the contents of `/db`, wherever our database lives. Of course, these data files are likely to be changing while they're being backed up, because the process itself can take minutes or hours depending on the size of the database.

Because of this, we call `pg_start_backup` to start the backup process. To begin with, it will commit pending writes to the database files (checkpoint). Afterwards, it will continue normal operation, but will also keep track of which transaction files were produced during the backup. This is important for future restores.

Next we invoke `pg_stop_backup` to complete the backup. This command not only finishes the backup, but also creates a file with a `.backup` extension that identifies the first and last archive logs necessary to restore the database to full working order. We need the first, last, and every transaction log in between to restore, which is what the last set of commands is for.

Knowing that the most recent `.backup` file archived by the database contains this information, we parse it using various Unix commands to identify every file between the first marked archive log, and the end of the backup itself. No file is older than the `.backup` file. All of these files are required to fully restore the database, and the process itself is fairly complicated.

We highly recommend implementing a more robust and tested version of the outlined steps, or using a preexisting backup library or third-party tool. For example, OmniPITR is often recommended. Our quick and dirty method works, but it should be fairly obvious why `pg_basebackup` automates and abstracts away most of the complexity in our example. We gain *flexibility* here, not ease of use.

There's more...

Now we should discuss exactly what kind of flexibility we may gain.

Parallel compression

Compressing files is very CPU intensive; `pigz` and `pbzip2` are still very handy, and `tar` works very well with external utilities. We can alter the archival command for the `/db` directory from the previous commands with the `-I` flag to choose our own compression program, as shown in the following command:

```
$> tar -c -I pigz -f backup.tar.gz /db
```

Alternatively, since `pigz` can take parameters for choosing the number of threads, or because certain versions of `tar` don't support the `-I` flag, we can send the output of `tar` to `pigz` instead by using the following command:

```
$> tar -c /db | pigz -p 4 > backup.tar.gz
```

Unlike `pg_basebackup`, these `tar` commands work with complex databases that make extensive use of tablespaces. Each tablespace can be handled separately and compressed in parallel, drastically reducing compression time.

Some may argue that `pg_basebackup` does support tablespaces, and it does create `.tar.gz` files for every user-created tablespace in the database along with `base.tar.gz`. However, the `tar` output format of this tool will not stream to standard output if there are user-created tablespaces. This means that our trick of capturing the stream with `pigz` would not work in such advanced systems. Hence, we used `tar` in this example.

Making a tar backup standby-ready

With PostgreSQL, a database in standby or streaming mode will not have its own transaction logs while recovery is in progress, since it uses some other source of archived transaction logs to apply changes to the database. This means that backing these files up is often excessive. Remember, we mentioned that `pg_basebackup` omits them by default for similar reasons. Thankfully, `tar` can also exclude them, or any other paths. Again, we will modify the `/db` backup command as follows:

```
$> tar -c -z -f backup.tar.gz --exclude=pg_xlog  /db
```

Now, if the `backup.tar.gz` file is uncompressed, it can only be used for standby or streaming replication.

Backing up tablespaces

We keep talking about tablespaces, but how do we handle them? PostgreSQL tablespaces reside in the `pg_tblspc` subdirectory of the `database` instance. To back these up separately, we want to tell `tar` to ignore them using the following command:

```
$> tar -c -z -f backup.tar.gz --exclude=pg_tblspc  /db
```

Now we can back up all of the tablespaces that live in that directory. Something like the following bash snippet could do the job nicely:

```
for f in $(find /db/pg_tblspc); do
    d=$(readlink -f $f)
    n=$(basename $f)
    tar -czf /backup/$n.tar.gz -C $d .
done
```

Each tablespace will be compressed in a separate file named after its database object identifier. Incidentally, this is exactly what `pg_basebackup` would do. But we can alter any of these commands as much as we desire. For instance, to introduce parallel compression we can use the following shell code:

```
for f in $(find /db/pg_tblspc); do
    d=$(readlink -f $f)
    n=$(basename $f)
    tar -C $d . -c | pigz -p 8 > /backup/$n.tar.gz
done
```

Now we can do something `pg_basebackup` can't, and use parallel compression on all tablespaces in the database instead of just the default compression. That is just one example of what we can modify within the backup process itself. It is a bit more work, but scripts can automate most or all of these extra steps.

Backing up archived transaction logs

Since our database is in `archive` mode, it may be producing archived transaction logs at a precipitous rate. If we want to do **point in time recovery** (**PITR**) or certain types of database standby, it is generally a good idea to preserve these to tape as well. For example, if executed at midnight, the following snippet of bash would compress the previous day's archived logs:

```
find /archive/ -type f -name '0000*' -mtime +0 ! \
        -printf '%f\n' >> /archive/MANIFEST
tar -C /archive/ --files-from=/archive/MANIFEST -c -I pigz \
        -f /backup/axlog.$(date -d '-1 day' +"%Y-%m-%d").tar.gz
find /archive/ -type f -name '0000*' -mtime +0 -delete
```

Now these backup files can be stored elsewhere for PITR restores. For very important databases, being able to use old backup files and transaction logs means that the database can be restored to any previous time since its creation. Always be sure to have access to old archive logs if this is a desired option.

Taking snapshots (Advanced)

Filesystem snapshots can provide a better-integrity guarantee for PostgreSQL backups, as files on a snapshot do not change during the backup. In Linux systems, the **Linux Volume Manager** (**LVM**) provides this capability. On BSD or specially altered Linux systems, ZFS is also available. On expensive SAN systems, this is often a built-in function. Due to its availability, we will cover LVM in this recipe.

Getting ready

Let's assume we have a 500 GB raw block device provided as `/dev/sdb`. This can be from an internal RAID or SAN management's LUN storage, or even just an internal disk. The following commands will make the `/db` path available to initialize as a new database:

```
$> pvcreate /dev/sdb
$> vgcreate db_group /dev/sdb
$> lvcreate -L 450G -n db_volume db_group
$> mkfs -t ext4 /dev/db_group/db_volume
$> mount /dev/db_group/db_volume /db
```

Please refer to the *Getting a basic export (Simple)* recipe on preparing a `sample` database.

How to do it...

With LVM in place, there are several new commands available to manage the volume itself. Let's back up the entire contents of the `/db` directory within a database snapshot using the following steps:

1. Start by creating a new snapshot volume:

   ```
   $> lvcreate -s -L 40G -n db_snap db_group/db_volume
   ```

2. Next, mount the directory so `tar` can copy the database files:

   ```
   $> mkdir /mnt/snap
   $> mount /dev/db_group/db_snap /mnt/snap
   ```

3. Now, perform a `tar` backup:

   ```
   $> tar -C /mnt/snap -c -z -f /backup/db_backup.tar.gz .
   ```

4. Finally, unmount and destroy the snapshot volume:

   ```
   $> umount /mnt/snap
   $> lvremove -f db_group/db_snap
   ```

How it works...

The process itself is basically a wrapper for whatever backup method we want to choose. During the setup, we create a physical volume that represents the actual device. On top of that goes the `volume` group, which allows us to group several devices or volumes together. Lastly comes the logical `volume` itself. We only allocate 450 GB of the total size, so we can use up to 50 GB for snapshots.

When a snapshot volume is created (`lvcreate -s`), it is tied to the named volume, and uses space in the same `volume` group. In this case, we used 40 GB of the available 50 GB. While the snapshot volume exists, any changed blocks on the source volume are written to this space instead. This means our example will allow up to 40 GB of data to change before the filesystem notices that the space is exhausted and it automatically deallocates the volume.

When we mount the snapshot volume, we actually see an unchanged copy of the `/db` directory, mounted at `/mnt/snap` instead. Our running applications see `/db` normally, so they can keep operating without interruption. This is why we direct the backup `tar` command to the snapshot mount and back up everything inside. This data is frozen in time, as if the database had simply stopped operating.

When the backup is finished, we simply unmount and remove the volume. This prevents possible problems from LVM destroying a full snapshot, and lets us reuse the space in subsequent backup operations.

This kind of backup doesn't need the `pg_start_backup` or `pg_stop_backup` commands, because no new transaction logs can be written in the snapshot, and nothing can be archived. The files we backed up can be extracted elsewhere and started as a separate database as if it had crashed while operating.

There's more...

It's easy to see that snapshots are very powerful, but there are several elements to keep in mind while using them.

Proper snapshot sizing

Why did we choose 40 GB for our snapshot volume? In our case, this was just an illustrative amount. In a real scenario, we would want to carefully calculate suitable snapshot sizes. This might simply be multiplying the average data turnover by the usual back up duration, and doubling that amount. We might also back up during a less active time of day (such as midnight) with a semi-large snapshot.

The point to remember is that the snapshot supplies all necessary space for any changed blocks on any file in the source volume, or any new files generated, such as transaction logs. The easiest way to see how much of this space is used, is to call some other LVM commands using the following command:

```
$> lvdisplay db_group/db_snap
```

The section entitled **Allocated to snapshot** shows how much of the volume is being used. Creating and monitoring a temporary snapshot is a good way to gauge the rate of data turnover before scheduling a real snapshot backup.

In our case, we reserved 10 percent of the total volume size, which is a good starting point. It is always possible to return excess space to the database volume with `lvextend` and `resize2fs`. To return 10 GB of space to the `db_volume` volume, we would adjust it while it is unmounted using the following commands:

```
$> umount /db
$> lvextend -L +10G db_group/db_volume
$> resize2fs /dev/db_group/db_volume
```

It is worth mentioning that ZFS has features that negate a lot of the work we performed previously. Unfortunately, properly setting up a good ZFS filesystem is a non-trivial exercise. We highly recommend obtaining a book that outlines how to best use this filesystem if you plan on utilizing this approach.

Snapshot backup targets

It may be tempting to back up the database to the source volume, as it's likely very large. This inclination must be ignored, however! Remember that any block written in the source volume comes from the snapshot. For very large databases, this could require hundreds of GB of space for the backup alone, ignoring any changes of the database itself.

Best practice suggests directing a backup to another device entirely. Larger systems commonly have a separate backup mount such as a NAS or SAN device where backups can reside in a vault area before being committed to tape for long-term storage. Not only is this safer for a snapshot, but much faster as well, since the backup is not stealing read or write throughput from the source volume.

The assumption through all of these examples is that `/backup` is a source volume. This is a good idea for all backup types, but is especially necessary for snapshot backups to avoid IO contention and snapshot destruction.

Each tablespace is likely to be held on a separate volume, and each would need a separate snapshot command. Even if this is done virtually simultaneously, there is a slight risk of a race condition between the different times for which each of the snapshots were frozen, leaving the data files backed up in an undetermined state. Any tables knocked out of sync due to this should be saved by replaying archive logs during recovery, but be wary of the limitations in this approach.

Synchronizing backup servers (Intermediate)

Binary backups with `tar` create an intermediate file for archival purposes. Instead, it might be better to back up directly to another server to have a full running backup. To do this, most administrators rely on `rsync`, which remotely synchronizes data between two servers. For low volume servers, this can be much faster than `tar` as well.

Getting ready

Please refer to the *Getting a basic export (Simple)* recipe on preparing a `sample` database.

Our server will be running in the `/db` directory on both systems. Make sure the path of the directory exists and is owned by the `postgres` user. On the remote server that will be receiving the backup, create a file named `/etc/rsyncd.conf` with the following content:

```
[db_sync]
    path = /db
    comment = DB Backup Server
    uid = postgres
    gid = postgres
    read only = false
    use chroot = true
```

There are other available options for securing the remote server, but for now, we will ignore those options for the purposes of demonstration.

How to do it...

Creating an `rsync` backup comes in three basic steps:

1. Begin by putting the database in `backup` mode:

   ```
   $> psql -c "SELECT pg_start_backup('label');" postgres
   ```

2. Next, use the `rsync` command to synchronize the contents of the two servers:

   ```
   $> rsync -a -v -z /db/ postgres@remote_server::db_sync
   ```

3. Finally, end `backup` mode:

   ```
   $> psql -c "SELECT pg_stop_backup();" postgres
   ```

How it works...

In our initial steps, we configure the `rsync` daemon with a module to accept file transfers. It's configured to run as the `postgres` user by default since that is a very common setup. We also enable symbolic links because PostgreSQL uses them extensively in tablespaces. We do not want to diverge too far from our copied server, so all paths should remain the same if possible.

As with a `tar` backup, we tell PostgreSQL that we're starting a backup. This is not strictly necessary since we're making an exact copy of the database as it runs, but is a good practice.

Next, we use `rsync` to physically copy the data to the remote server. We add the `-a` flag to copy all data attributes such as file ownership and permissions. The `-v` flag is simply to increase verbosity so we can watch the copy progress. Again, such a flag is not necessary but useful for illustrative purposes.

> To shorten the duration of the backup and lower the amount of transaction log files, you will need to track and execute the same command before starting `backup` mode. The `rsync` command will then only copy changed files since the first synchronization.

Finally, we stop the backup. If we never entered PostgreSQL's `backup` mode, we don't need to end it either. In reality, the entire backup can be done with the `rsync` command alone.

> The `rsync` command does not need to work on a push model. Instead, the `rsyncd.conf` file could reside on the server itself, and backup servers could fetch files from the master copy. This may even be the suggested method if there are several backup servers that need to be updated asynchronously.

There's more...

If we check the manual page for `rsync`, we can see that there are several other highly useful switches that can modify or control the data stream. There are a lot of useful switches to discuss.

Speeding up rsync

The `rsync` command operates in real time, but before it starts, it makes a list of all files that need to be copied. Since the database is running while we are copying its contents, new files may appear during the backup that will not get copied, and old files may vanish. The best way to use `rsync` is to actually run it multiple times with an extra parameter as shown in the following commands:

```
$> rsync -a -v -z /db/ postgres@remote_server::db_sync
$> rsync -a -v -z --delete-after /db/ postgres@remote_server::db_sync
```

The first command may not complete for several hours depending on the database size, so the second should be executed once or twice to drastically shorten the number of changed files we need to copy.

Afterwards, it's good practice to shut down the database, and do one final sync. This guarantees that no files have changed and the backup is fully valid. Because we ran earlier synchronizations, downtime should be very short.

Whole file sync

PostgreSQL keeps most table data in 1 GB chunks. To avoid recopying data, `rsync` will normally compute differences between files on each server. This can actually take a very long time for such large files. If enough bandwidth is available, it may actually be easier to simply transfer the whole file than the differing parts using the following command:

```
$> rsync -W -a -v -z /db/ postgres@remote_server::db_sync
```

The `-W` flag does exactly this.

Exclude transaction logs

If we set up a backup copy for replication, we do not need the `pg_xlog` directory, so we can exclude that as well.

```
$> rsync -a -v -z --exclude=pg_xlog /db/ \
  postgres@remote_server::db_sync
```

Restoring a binary backup (Simple)

We have now discussed several different methods for obtaining a binary backup. What do we actually do with these binary backup files? We'll cover a simple restore since there is no supplied utility that performs this task.

Getting ready

Please refer to the *Getting a basic export (Simple)* recipe to bootstrap our `sample` database. Then, we want a very simple backup to restore. We should stop the database to avoid any extra work using the following commands:

```
$> pg_ctl -D /db/pgdata stop -m fast
$> tar -C /db/pgdata --exclude=pg_xlog -cz \
  -f /db/backup/backup.tar.gz .
$> tar -C /db/pgdata/pg_xlog --exclude=archive_status \
  --exclude=archive_status -czf /db/backup/xlog.tar.gz .
```

Once these files are safely stored, erase our sample database using the following command:

```
$> rm -Rf /db/pgdata
```

How to do it...

Restoring a binary backup is generally easy if we run a few commands as the `postgres` user, as shown in the following list:

1. First, create a directory and extract the backup file to that location:

    ```
    $> mkdir -m 700 /db/pgdata
    $> tar -C /db/pgdata -xzf /db/backup/backup.tar.gz
    ```

2. Then, create a directory for the archive logs to restore. We also need the `pg_xlog` directory which the PostgreSQL expects for the database to start properly. Once these directories are created, uncompress the transaction logs we backed up:

    ```
    $> mkdir -m 700 /db/pgdata/{archived,pg_xlog}
    $> tar -C /db/pgdata/archived -xzf /db/backup/xlog.tar.gz
    ```

3. Finally, create a file named `recovery.conf` in the `/db/pgdata` directory to contain the following:

    ```
    restore_command = 'cp /db/pgdata/archived/%f "%p"'
    ```

4. Then start the database as usual. It will recover for a period of time and become available:

    ```
    $> pg_ctl -D /db/pgdata start
    ```

How it works...

We cheat a little to create a simple restore backup that will require using a `recovery.conf` file. All recovery is controlled through this file, so it is important to know how it works.

Afterwards, we simply create the basic directory for the database as it existed before, and extract the backup file there. When a database is in recovery, it copies old transaction logs and processes them, ensuring the database properly reflects all the necessary data.

The real trick here is the `recovery.conf` file, which plays a central role in almost all binary recovery. We used one of the simplest settings to copy transaction logs to their required destination directory, and before this is all over, we will learn much more. For now, know that in the `restore_command` line, `%f` is the name of a file PostgreSQL needs, and `%p` is where the file should reside.

This means we could use any equivalent Unix command instead of our simple copy. For instance, we could use `rsync` to copy the file from a remote storage location instead.

There's more...

Restoring a simple backup is effectively just extraction and recovery. We don't even need a bootstrap like with a SQL restore. However, there is still a little more to know.

No extract for rsync backups

If we use `rsync` to copy files from another server instead, we have an exact copy of the database as if it were never stopped. In this case, there is no backup file to extract, and no other files to restore. We don't really need a `recovery.conf` file for the database to start either.

> Do not exclude the `pg_xlog` directory in your `rsync` command if you plan to do this, as PostgreSQL requires those files to start the database. It is also good practice to only resync data when the server is stopped so that the data files are consistent.

Remote data copies

The copy command can be anything we want. It is good practice to have a vault server that acts as a backup target. Let's set up a `recovery.conf` that copies data from a remote server instead.

```
restore_command = 'rsync -a postgres@backup_server::archive/%f "%p"'
```

This assumes that we have `rsync` installed, and have an equivalent `rsyncd.conf` on the `backup` server. We could also use `scp` instead for a secure SSH-based copy, or we could execute our own pre-written script.

> Be careful with `scp`. It copies files over without an intermediate temporary name, so the recovering database may try to read a file while it is being transferred. A safer option is to use the (`--rsh=ssh`) `rsync` switch to use `ssh` as a transport mechanism only. This way, your data is still protected by `ssh`, without potentially damaging the `backup` server.

Again, this is just one possible alternative available. A good environment makes use of several techniques as appropriate.

Point in time recovery (Intermediate)

PostgreSQL also has the ability to restore the database to any point in history following the previous backup. This is called **point in time recovery** (**PITR**). It does this by keeping files called transaction logs. So long as we store these transaction logs, we can use them to restore to any date they contain.

Getting ready

Please refer to the *Getting a basic export (Simple)* recipe to bootstrap our database. Before we start the database to create the `sample` database, we need to change a couple of settings in `postgresql.conf`. For this, we will need a path in `/archive` to store transaction logs, which can be used by the following configuration settings:

```
wal_level = archive
archive_mode = on
archive_command = 'test -f /archive/%f || cp %p /archive/%f'
```

Then start the database and use `pgbench` to initialize our sample data. Afterwards, we need a very simple backup to restore. Leave the database running for the following steps:

```
$> psql -c "SELECT pg_start_backup('label');" postgres
$> tar -C /db/pgdata --exclude=pg_xlog -cz \
            -f /db/backup/backup.tar.gz .
$> psql -c "SELECT pg_stop_backup();" postgres
```

After the backup, we want to generate a bit more activity that we can ignore. Make a note of the time, then run the following commands to erase the `teller` table so that we can restore to a point before that happened:

```
$> psql -c "drop table pgbench_tellers; " sample
$> psql -c "select pg_switch_xlog(); " sample
```

Once these files are safely stored, stop and erase our `sample` database:

```
$> pg_ctl -D /db/pgdata stop -m fast
$> rm -Rf /db/pgdata
```

How to do it...

At first, our restore works as before. Assume that the time of our backup was 5:15:26 P.M. on February 15, 2013, and we know the table was dropped at 5:30:00 P.M. Remember to use the actual backup and drop times if following along. The following are the steps:

1. Create proper database folders, and extract the backup from the previously stated database using the following commands:

    ```
    $> mkdir -m 700 /db/pgdata
    $> mkdir -m 700 /db/pgdata/pg_xlog
    $> tar -C /db/pgdata -xzf /db/backup/backup.tar.gz
    ```

2. Then create a file named `recovery.conf` in our `/db/pgdata` directory to contain the following:

```
restore_command = 'cp /archive/%f "%p"'
recovery_target_time = '2012-02-15 17:29:00'
```

3. Then start the database as usual. It will recover for a few minutes until it reaches the indicated time, and become available.

```
$> pg_ctl -D /db/pgdata start
```

How it works...

Most of the changes necessary for point in time recovery to work are handled before we even start the database. In our preparation, we set the database `wal_level` to archive. This forces PostgreSQL to write extra information to transaction logs so this type of recovery works.

We also didn't stop the database during the backup process. This means we really should use the `pg_start_backup` and `pg_stop_backup` commands to ensure all of the necessary transaction logs are written to the `/archive` directory.

With a backup, we then connect to the database to drop the `teller` table to simulate an accident. By calling `pg_switch_xlogs`, this information is also recorded to the archives. This way, we can prove that the selected time was honored by our recovery.

Recovery itself is tied to `recovery.conf`, which tells the database to recover from our `/archive` directory until the indicated time. Note how this is probably the most straightforward part of the operation. Knowing where to find the archived transaction log files and putting the database in the proper write mode are the real keys to PITR.

In the example `recovery_target_time`, we restore to one minute before the table was dropped. This way, we can save the contents of the table and reimport them into our main database.

There's more...

With the ability to choose the time when recovery stops, there are other methods of stopping recovery.

Named restore points

If we are doing work known to possibly be dangerous, it is best to do it within a transaction. But larger sweeping changes may contain a lot of DDL or precede a large series of database loading jobs. At these times, it may be beneficial to name certain actions so we can recover specifically to a point before they executed. To do this, we first need to name the action with a built-in function.

```
$> psql -c "select pg_create_restore_point('dangerous');" postgres
```

Then after the commands are executed and we decide to restore to our named label, our `recovery.conf` changes slightly as shown in the following settings:

```
restore_command = 'cp /archive/%f "%p"'
recovery_target_name = 'dangerous'
```

With no other changes in the process, recovery will stop when it reaches the named point we created.

Timelines

At some point at the end of the recovery, the database will output the following line to the log file:

```
LOG:   selected new timeline ID: 2
```

What is a timeline? By restoring a database, we are effectively traveling in time, to the period when the backup was taken. This is especially true if we restore to a specific point in time or a named restore point. If this is done several different times, we may want to recover to a timeline somewhere in the middle of several recovery attempts. We can do that by selecting a timeline in the `recovery.conf` file.

```
restore_command = 'cp /archive/%f "%p"'
recovery_target_timeline = 4
```

This type of recovery will restore to the end of the selected timeline unless a time is specified. In the previous case, we did a lot of select statements and came to the conclusion that it was the correct timeline, and we want it to fully recover before using it as our main database.

It is important to remember that no recovery can reach a time before the backup was taken. In addition, all transaction logs after the backup are necessary to be fully restored. At the very least, we need the logs leading to our selected time, timeline, or recovery point. That is why we keep them in a remote server or tape for as long as possible. Enterprise systems sometimes keep both backups and transaction log files around for several years. Either way, it is good practice to keep both binary backup types for emergency use for several days.

Warm and hot standby restore (Intermediate)

Another option for restoring a PostgreSQL backup is to restore indefinitely. A backup restored this way would always be a working copy of the database, available with a single activation command (`warm`), or online for read-only queries (`hot`).

Getting ready

Please refer to the *Getting a basic export (Simple)* recipe to bootstrap our database. Before we start the server to create the `sample` database, we need to change a few settings in `postgresql.conf` as shown in the following code:

```
wal_level = hot_standby
archive_mode = on
archive_command = 'rsync -a %p postgres@backup::archive/%f'
```

Next, we will want to set up the `backup` server with an `rsyncd.conf` file:

```
[db_sync]
    path = /db/pgdata
    comment = DB Backup Server
    uid = postgres
    gid = postgres
    read only = false
    use chroot = true
  [archive]
    path = /db/archive
    comment = Archived Transaction Logs
    uid = postgres
    gid = postgres
    read only = false
    use chroot = true
```

Make sure `/db/pgdata` and `/db/archive` exist on both servers and the `rsync` daemon has been restarted. Then start the main database and use `pgbench` to initialize our sample data.

How to do it...

The `rsync` backup step that we will perform also acts as a restore. The data on the backup server will be almost ready to run. Execute the following commands from the main database server:

1. Start by entering `backup` mode:

   ```
   $> psql -c "SELECT pg_start_backup('standby');" postgres
   ```

2. Next, send the `data` files to the `backup` server:

   ```
   $> rsync -a --exclude=pg_xlog /db/pgdata/ \
    postgres@backup::db_sync
   ```

3. Then close `backup` mode:

```
$> psql -c "SELECT pg_stop_backup();" postgres
```

Once the data is copied, go to the `backup` server and finish setting up the database. Remember, this is on the backup server, not the primary server. The following are the steps to finish the setup:

1. Create a `pg_xlog` directory so the database will start:

```
$> mkdir /db/pgdata/pg_xlog
```

2. Remove the `backup` label, since it is not necessary for recovery:

```
$> rm /db/pgdata/backup_label
```

3. The `postmaster` files are created during operation for bookkeeping, and can cause problems when restarting if certain flags are omitted. Remove them:

```
$> rm /db/pgdata/postmaster.*
```

4. Create a `recovery.conf` file on the `backup` server with the following contents:

```
standby_mode = on
trigger_file = '/tmp/promote_db'
restore_command = 'cp -f /db/archive/%f "%p"'
```

5. Then start the backup copy of the database:

```
$> pg_ctl -D /db/pgdata start
```

How it works...

We are starting to combine many of the techniques we have learned so far. Primary among those is the ability to copy data from one server to another without the intermediate step of first transforming it to a single file.

We start the process by setting up the main server to produce transaction logs in `hot_standby` mode. Doing so is necessary if we want to utilize the database in read-only mode on the backup server. We also modify the `archive` command to transfer archived transaction logs directly to the `backup` server. This is just one method of doing so, though a fairly convenient one.

Having both of the `rsync` target paths set up in advance promotes these types of transfers. Data synchronization is necessary for starting the backup from scratch any time, and we need the archive log target so that the backup can stay in recovery mode.

The backup and restore process itself is something we covered before. Here, we simply copy all of the data from the main database except for the transaction logs. Those will be copied by the database using the `recovery.conf` file that controls the restore process. That recovery should begin as soon as the backup copy of the database is started.

With this setup, if we should try to connect to the backup database, it will respond with:

```
psql: FATAL:  the database system is starting up
```

That's okay for now, because we know the database is properly in recovery mode and keeping itself as a fresh backup of our main copy. This status is what's known as warm standby, and for a very long time, was the only way PostgreSQL could do standby operations.

There's more...

Simply having a standby database is a very powerful backup technique. But how do we actually utilize the backup copy?

Trigger a backup online

The easiest method for activating the `backup` database so it acts as the main database would, is to use a `trigger` file. This can actually be activated by any user who can access the backup server. In our `recovery.conf`, we defined a `trigger` file:

```
trigger_file = '/tmp/promote_db'
```

If this `trigger` file exists, PostgreSQL will delete it, stop processing transaction logs, and restart the database as a normal operating server. On secure dedicated backup servers, this is a valid and easy way for activating a `backup` server and making it a normal online database.

Backup database promotion

The second method utilizes another built-in capability of the venerable `pg_ctl` tool. To restart without a `trigger` file, we do something called a database promotion using the following command:

```
$> pg_ctl -D /db/pgdata promote
```

This has the same effect as the `trigger` file, but can only be used by the user who started or owns the PostgreSQL service. On less secure servers, it might be a good idea to use the previous command instead of the `trigger_file` line in the `recovery.conf` file.

Hot standby

Believe it or not, a `standby` server does not simply have to process transaction logs and wait to be promoted or triggered. In fact, it is now very common to run one or more backup servers for various purposes related to load balancing.

To make a backup database readable, simply modify its `postgresql.conf` file and enable `hot_standby`:

```
hot_standby = on
```

So long as the main database also has the `wal_level` set to `hot_standby`, and had that setting before the backup was taken, backup databases can also service read-only queries.

Asynchronous archival

In some ways, using `rsync` as the `archive_command` line is a bad practice. If there are multiple backup or standby servers, where should the transaction logs be sent? There's also a small risk that the target becomes unresponsive and files build up waiting for archival until they consume all available drive space.

Another way to ensure that the archive logs make it to the `backup` server is to utilize the Unix `cron` system. Let's make a `cron` entry on the main database server for the `postgres` user by calling `crontab -e`:

```
* * * * *  rsync -a /db/archive/ postgres@backup::archive
```

This will check every minute, and ensure that the `/db/archive` directories are the same on both servers. Of course, for this to work, we should revert to the old `archive_command` in `postgresql.conf`:

```
archive_command = 'test -f /db/archive/%f || cp %p /db/archive/%f'
```

With this in place, PostgreSQL will archive old transaction log files locally, and an asynchronous background process will ensure that these files reach the `backup` server eventually.

> You can set up the synchronization job on the `backup` server instead, and reverse the direction of the `rsync`, so the `backup` server pulls the files from the primary database. By doing this, you can set up multiple backup servers for different purposes.

It is a good idea to also set up a cleanup process to prune very old transaction log files. Having an asynchronous transmission method is safer, but a little more difficult to maintain. We can use `cron` similarly to the `rsync` to do this:

```
0 * * * * find /db/archive -type f -mtime +7 -delete
```

This would delete any transaction log files older than one week, every hour.

Streaming replication (Advanced)

The last topic we are going to cover is a newer method for indefinite binary recovery over a network connection known as **streaming replication**. A backup restored this way would always be a working copy of the database, and does not require third-party tools like `rsync` to utilize. Being always online, this is a perfect candidate for disaster recovery scenarios instead of merely pure backup availability.

Getting ready

Please refer to the *Getting a basic export (Simple)* recipe to bootstrap our database. Before we start the server to create the `sample` database, we need to change a few settings in `postgresql.conf` using the following code:

```
wal_level = hot_standby
max_wal_senders = 5
```

Then we must allow a user to connect from the `backup` server to the `replication` database. For this example, assume the `backup` server has the IP address `192.168.5.5`. We activate it by adding the following line to `pg_hba.conf`:

```
host replication replication 192.168.5.5/32 trust
```

Then start the main database and use `pgbench` to initialize our sample data. Afterwards, we should actually create the `replication` user and give it the ability to use system replication as shown in the following command:

```
$> psql -c "create user replication with replication;"
```

How to do it...

The `pg_basebackup` backup step, which we will perform on the `backup` server, also acts as a restore. The data on the backup server will be almost ready to run. The following are the steps for streaming applications:

1. Assuming that the main database resides at `192.168.5.1`, execute the following command from the `backup` database server:

   ```
   $> pg_basebackup -D /db/pgdata -h 192.168.5.1 -U replication
   ```

2. Next, create a `recovery.conf` file on the `backup` server with the following content:

   ```
   standby_mode = on
   trigger_file = '/tmp/promote_db'
   primary_conninfo = 'host=192.168.5.1 port=5432 user=replication'
   ```

3. Next, it's common practice to modify `postgresql.conf` to allow online read-only queries. Let's do that next using the following code snippet:

```
hot_standby = on
```

4. Then start the backup copy of the database:

```
$> pg_ctl -D /db/pgdata start
```

How it works...

What we have just created here is the default type of backup replication known as **asynchronous streaming replication**. It took a lot of extra preparation on the main database server to get this working.

We started by changing the `wal_level` database to `hot_standby` so the `backup` server can run in read-only mode. Also it is important that we set `max_wal_senders` to a non-zero value so the `backup` server can connect to the main database and request transaction files directly from the source. Because of this, we no longer need `rsync` at all, or even PostgreSQL `archive_mode`. Transferring files between both servers is only necessary as a safe fallback method in case the backup server cannot connect to the main database for some reason.

The `replication` database is actually a pseudo-database that does not actually exist. The line we placed in `pg_hba.conf` tells PostgreSQL that the `replication` user can connect to this pseudo-database from the `backup` server. Oddly enough, using `all` to indicate all databases actually does not work. To use replication, not only does a user with the `replication` permission need to exist, but they must be able to explicitly connect to the `replication` database. We admit that this might be somewhat confusing.

With all of this preparation out of the way, we revisit the `pg_basebackup` tool once more. Because the `replication` user can connect directly to the main database, it can actually create a copy of the database as well. In fact, that is the primary purpose of the `pg_basebackup` tool. Instead of copying transaction log files, it requests primary database files and saves them as a mirror of the source database.

The next step is to create a `recovery.conf` file to control how the backup copy acts. In our case, we want the usual `standby_mode`, a basic `trigger_file` to allow local promotion, and the real magic of streaming replication, that is, `primary_conninfo`. This is where we designate the connection string to the main database server. If everything works properly, the `backup` server will report the following in its logs after we start it:

```
LOG:  streaming replication successfully connected to primary
```

There's more...

Asynchronous replication is not the only option available for a `backup` server. We can also operate synchronously or use the backup copy of the database to produce backup files for long term storage.

Synchronous backup

Asynchronous backup is good for most cases. However, for mission-critical data that absolutely must exist on at least two servers before being saved at all, there is another option. Synchronous replication modifies the main database server in such a way that no transactions will commit at all unless at least one backup server also receives the data. To use this, we need to add a setting to the `postgresql.conf` file on our main server as shown in the following code:

```
synchronous_standby_names = 'backup_server'
```

We also need to append an `application_name` name to the end of the `primary_conninfo` setting to name our backup server:

```
primary_conninfo = '... application_name=backup_server'
```

Once we restart both the main and backup databases, transactions will presumably reflect increased durability.

Synchronous backup caveates

Though synchronous backup is more durable since all transactions must pass through at least two systems, PostgreSQL is very serious about honoring that data guarantee. If the `backup` server disconnects from the main server, either through server maintenance or network disruption, the main database will actually stop processing transactions entirely until the `backup` server returns to normal operation.

The only way to prevent this behavior is to temporarily disable synchronous replication in `postgresql.conf`:

```
synchronous_standby_names = ''
```

And then telling the server to reload:

```
$> pg_ctl -D /db/pgdata reload
```

This should be done before maintenance on the `backup` server, or if a network outage is detected between the two servers.

We also need to consider the effect of network latency. Because transactions must be acknowledged by two servers, locks are held longer on the main server. For non-critical data in a synchronous replication setup, clients should disable synchronous mode. This can be done with a basic PostgreSQL client command. The following sample update would not use synchronous replication:

```
SET synchronous_commit TO false;
UPDATE my_table
       SET modified_date = NOW()
  WHERE row_val LIKE '%change%';
```

The `synchronous_commit` setting can be used anywhere normal SQL is allowed. This is only a temporary change, and only applies to the current client connection. To reactivate synchronous commit in the same connection, it needs to be explicitly re-enabled using the following code:

```
SET synchronous_commit TO true;
```

Finally, we should note that synchronous replication only guarantees transactions that have been *received* by the `backup` server, not that they have been processed. Synchronous mode is really just a shallow extension of asynchronous, and as a consequence, retains many of the same limitations. One of those limits is that the backup server can only note that it has the transaction, not the progress of applying it.

In practice, backup servers usually apply transactions much faster than the main server because they do not generally carry the same transaction overhead. We just do not want to be unpleasantly surprised by an unexpected race condition if the two servers get out of sync.

Streaming backups

Probably the best use for a hot-standby or streaming backup is the ability to use it as the primary backup source. In all likelihood, the primary database is much busier than the backup or disaster recovery server. There are just a few things we need to remember:

- The database is only available for reading.
- As a consequence, `pg_basebackup` cannot be used. This restriction is removed in PostgreSQL 9.2 and above.
- Using `pg_start_backup` or `pg_stop_backup` are also not allowed. Again, PostgreSQL 9.2 and above make this possible.

This means `tar` and `rsync` style backups are good for older installs, with or without filesystem snapshots. `pg_dumpall` and `pg_dump` are also perfectly valid, since they only obtain read locks on the database while they operate.

Any of the previously mentioned backup methods that do not involve `pg_basebackup` can be used with very little modification. The easiest way is to simply stop the backup copy, since it is likely non-critical. Since the `backup` server is probably under less duress, parallel compression can utilize more available CPUs, and disk bandwidth saturation carries less operational risks.

The ultimate backup method is to have an entirely separate backup server to act in a disaster recovery role. Not only can it fill in for the main database in case of an outage, but low priority work and maintenance procedures such as regular backups can be offloaded without risking the primary system. Streaming replication makes this both easy and convenient.

Thank you for buying
Instant PostgreSQL Backup and Restore How-to

About Packt Publishing

Packt, pronounced 'packed', published its first book "*Mastering phpMyAdmin for Effective MySQL Management*" in April 2004 and subsequently continued to specialize in publishing highly focused books on specific technologies and solutions.

Our books and publications share the experiences of your fellow IT professionals in adapting and customizing today's systems, applications, and frameworks. Our solution based books give you the knowledge and power to customize the software and technologies you're using to get the job done. Packt books are more specific and less general than the IT books you have seen in the past. Our unique business model allows us to bring you more focused information, giving you more of what you need to know, and less of what you don't.

Packt is a modern, yet unique publishing company, which focuses on producing quality, cutting-edge books for communities of developers, administrators, and newbies alike. For more information, please visit our website: www.packtpub.com.

Writing for Packt

We welcome all inquiries from people who are interested in authoring. Book proposals should be sent to author@packtpub.com. If your book idea is still at an early stage and you would like to discuss it first before writing a formal book proposal, contact us; one of our commissioning editors will get in touch with you.

We're not just looking for published authors; if you have strong technical skills but no writing experience, our experienced editors can help you develop a writing career, or simply get some additional reward for your expertise.

PostgreSQL 9 Admin Cookbook

ISBN: 978-1-849510-28-8   Paperback: 360 pages

Solve real-world PostgreSQL problems with over 100 simple, yet incredibly effective recipes

1. Administer and maintain a healthy database

2. Monitor your database ensuring that it performs as quickly as possible

3. Tips for backup and recovery of your database

PostgreSQL Server Programming

ISBN: 978-1-849516-98-3   Paperback: 234 pages

Extend PostgreSQL and integrate the database layer into your development framework

1. Understand the extension framework of PostgreSQL, and leverage it in ways that you haven't even invented yet

2. Write functions, create your own data types, all in your favourite programming language

3. Step-by-step tutorial with plenty of tips and tricks to kick-start server programming

Please check **www.PacktPub.com** for information on our titles

Network Backup with Bacula How-To

ISBN: 978-1-849519-84-7   Paperback: 56 pages

Create an autonomous backup solution for your computer network using practical, hands-on recipes

1. Learn something new in an Instant! A short, fast, focused guide delivering immediate results.

2. Set up Bacula infrastructure.

3. Back up data and directories

4. Work with multiple-storage systems

PostgreSQL 9.0 High Performance

ISBN: 978-1-849510-30-1   Paperback: 468 pages

Accelerate your PostgreSQL system and avoid the common pitfalls that can slow it down

1. Learn the right techniques to obtain optimal PostgreSQL database performance, from initial design to routine maintenance

2. Discover the techniques used to scale successful database installations

3. Avoid the common pitfalls that can slow your system down

Please check **www.PacktPub.com** for information on our titles

36630635R00032

Made in the USA
Lexington, KY
29 October 2014